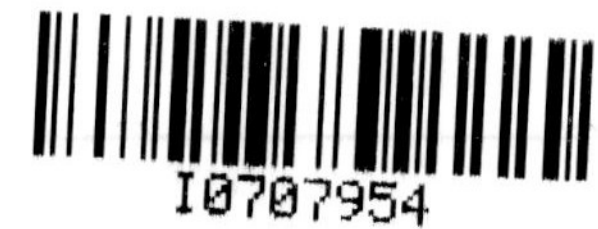

This home belongs to:

____

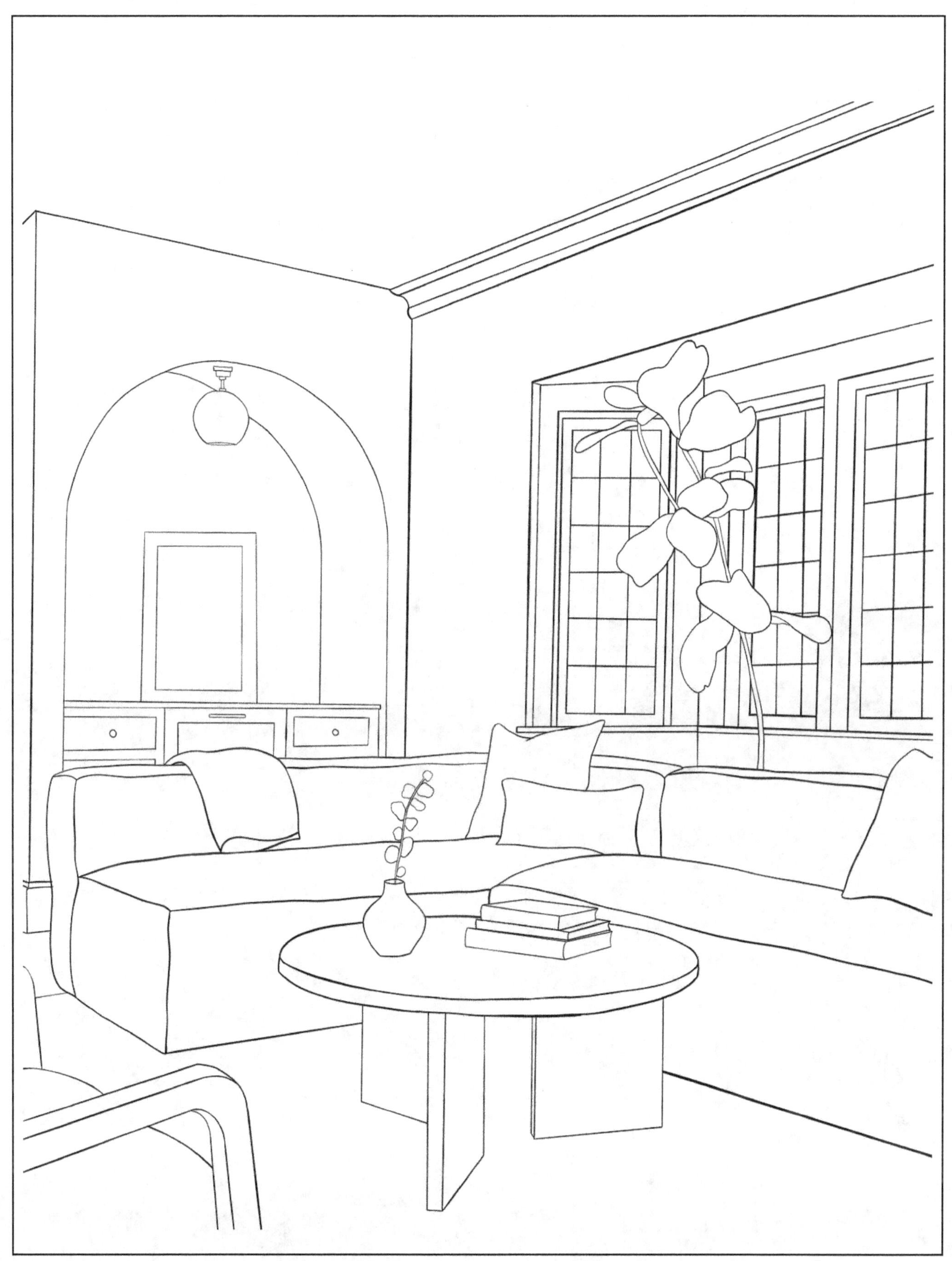

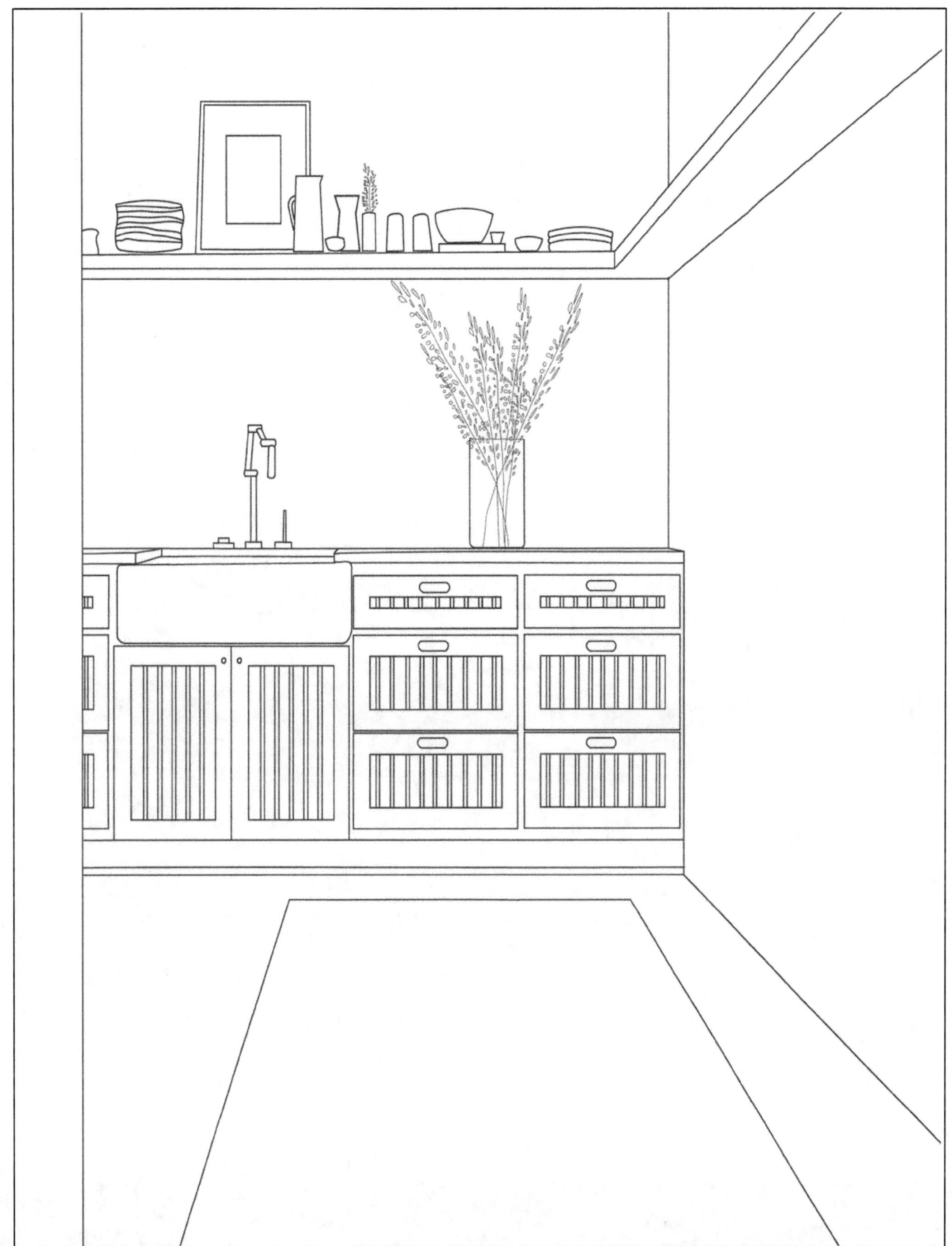

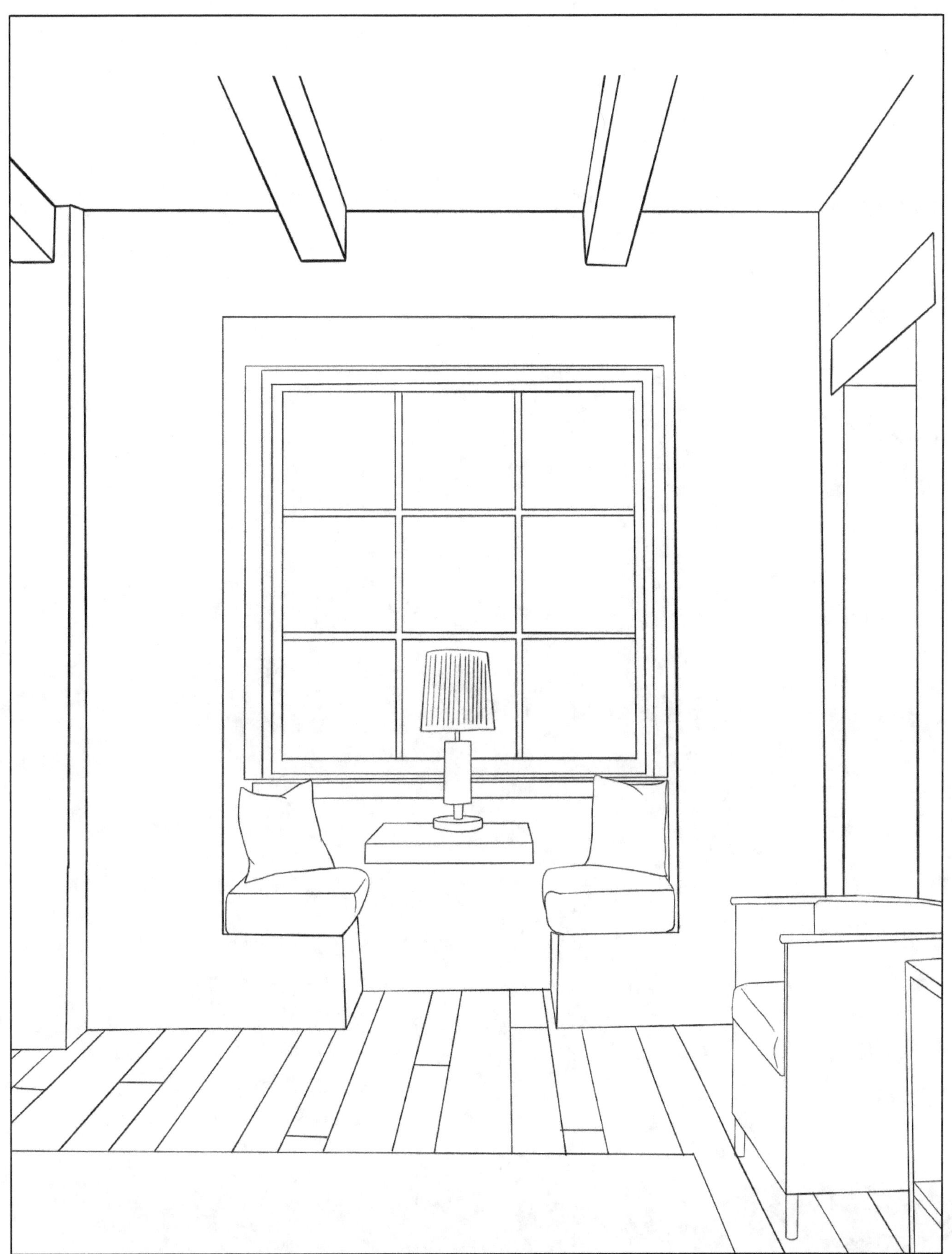

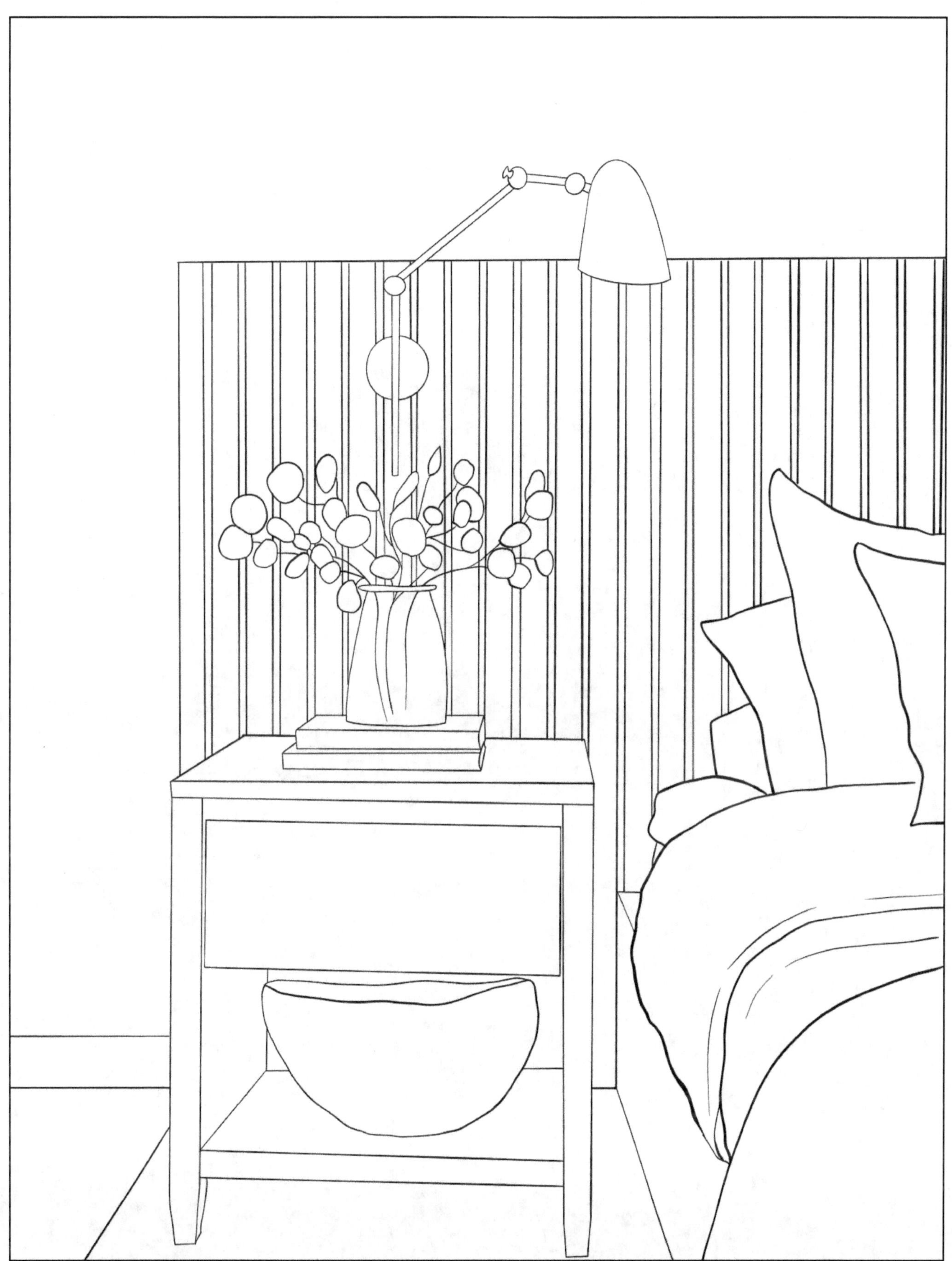

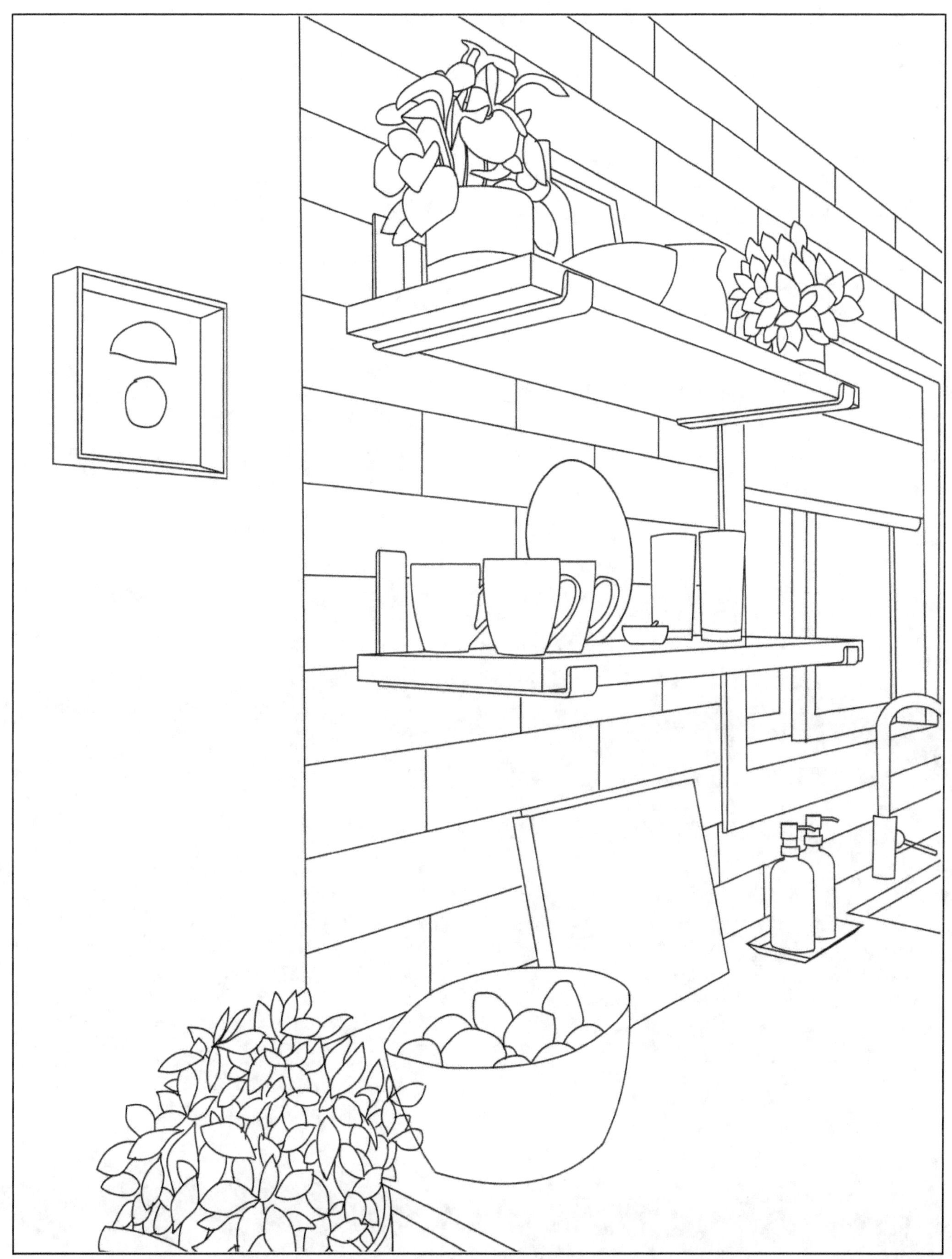

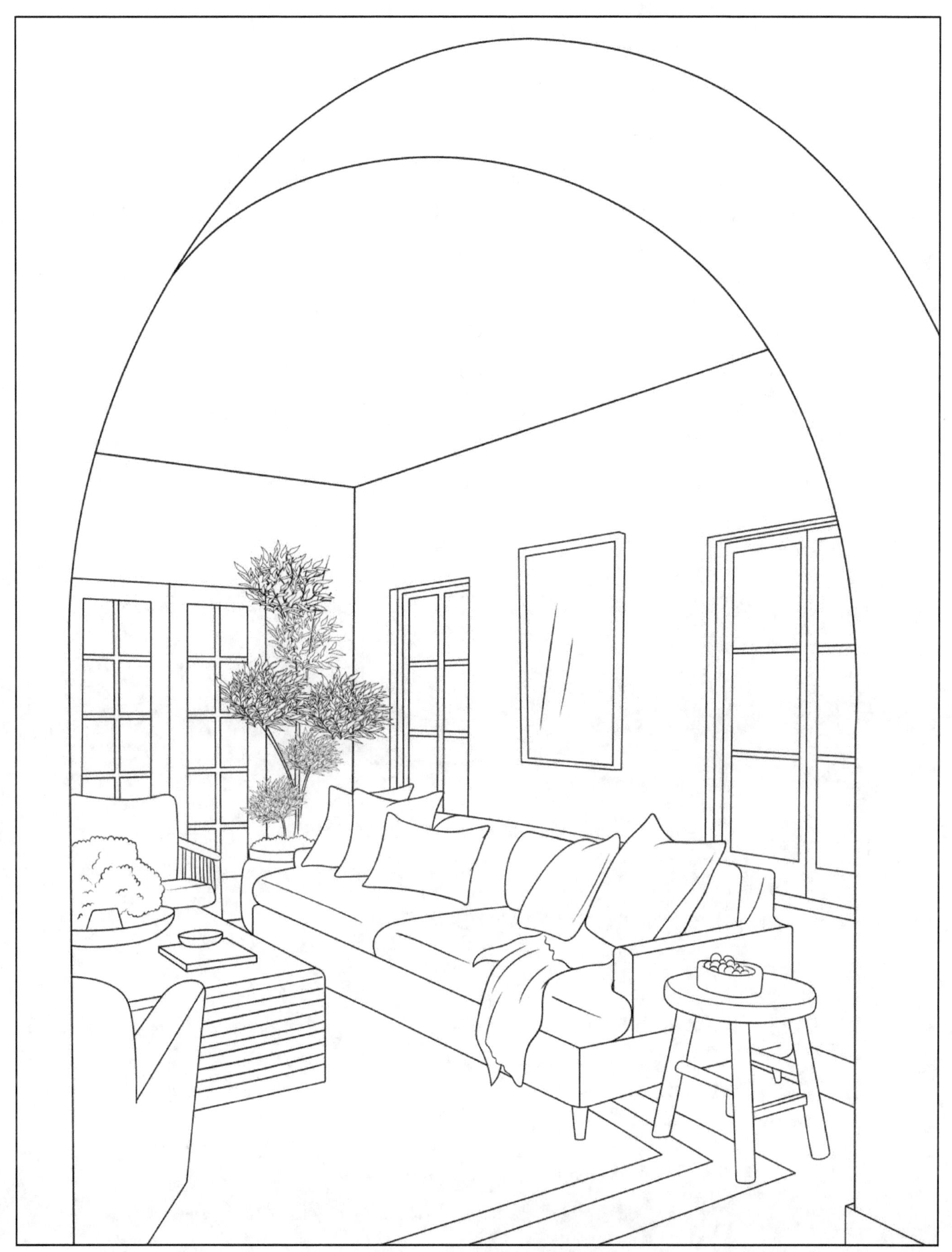

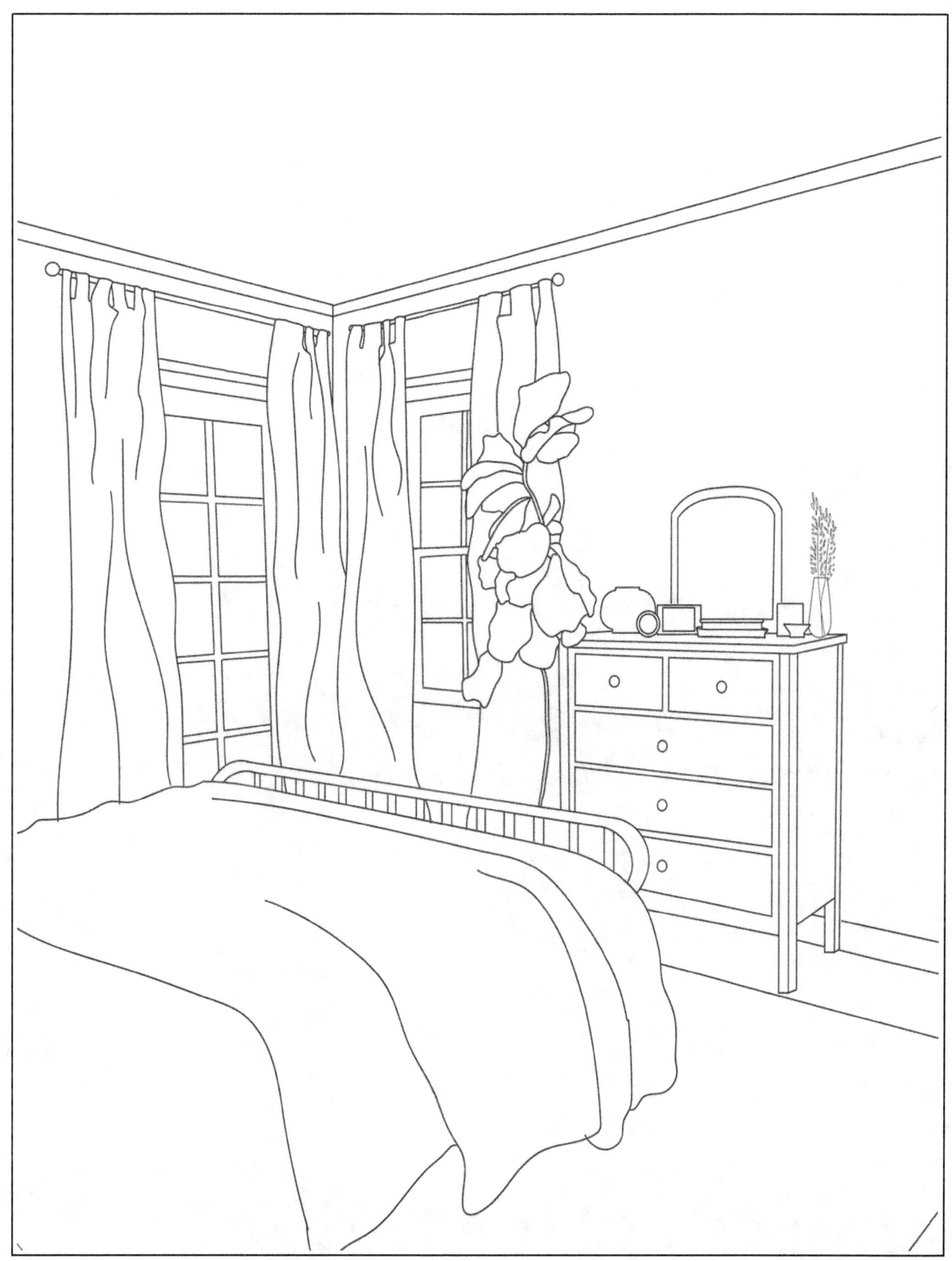

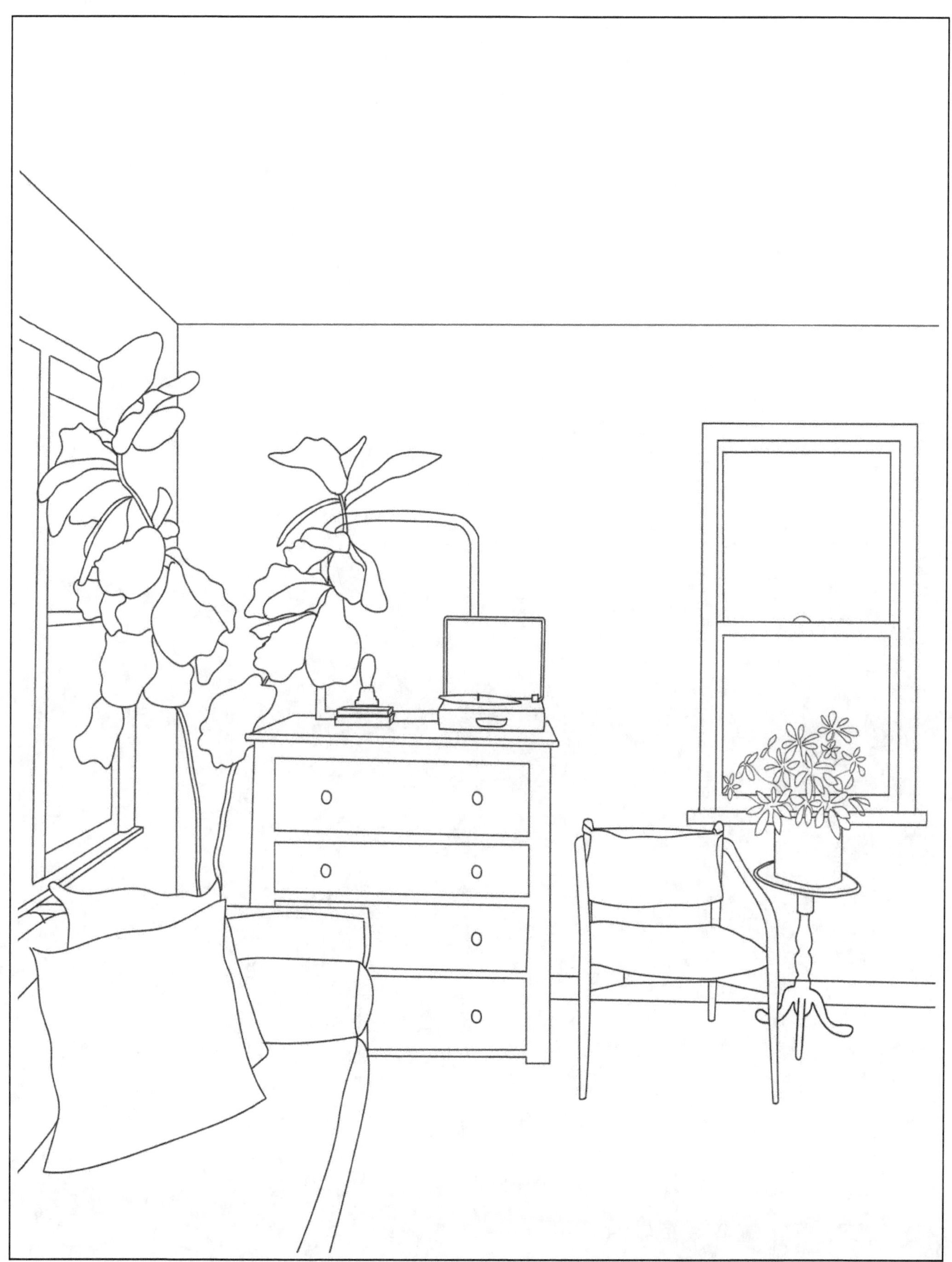

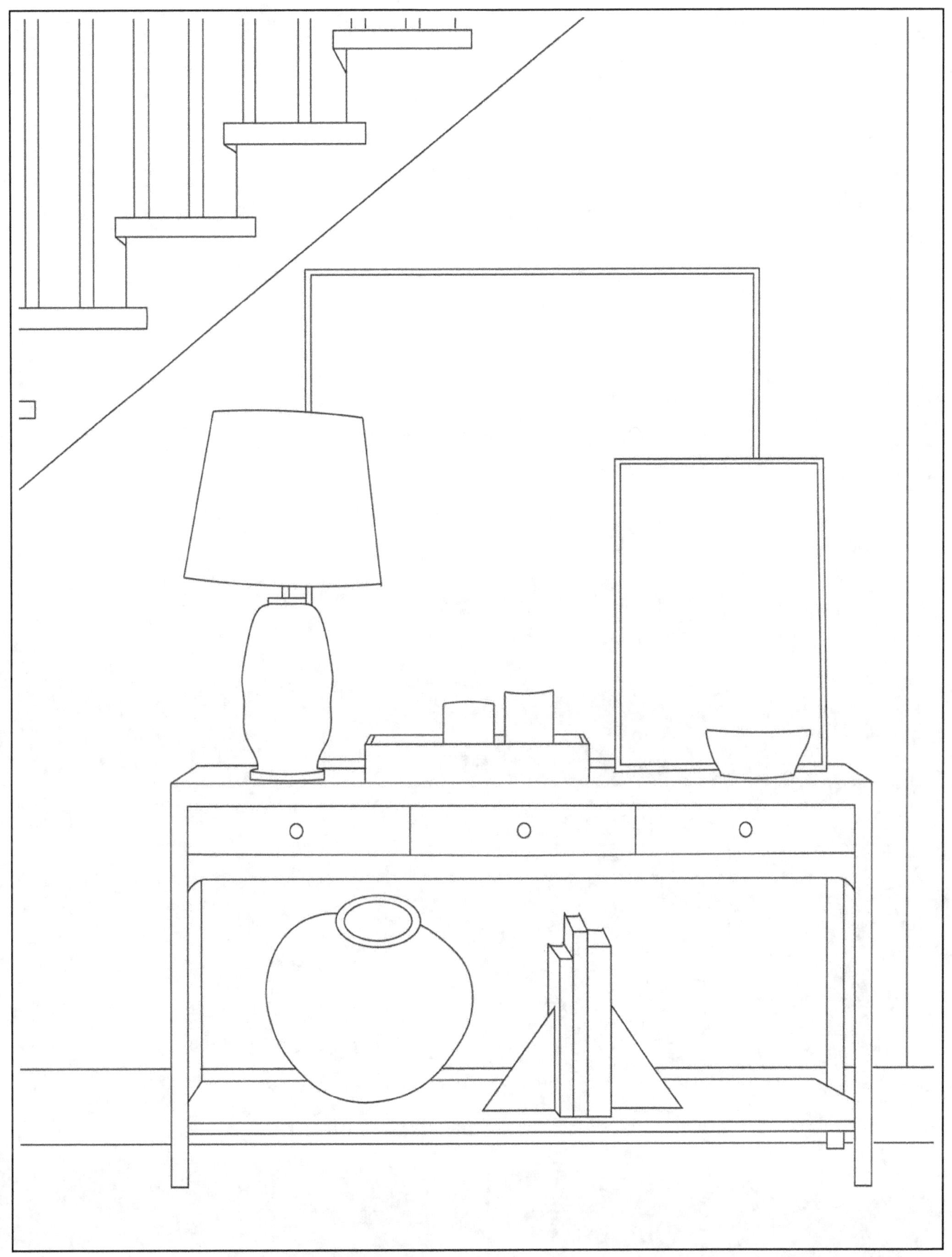

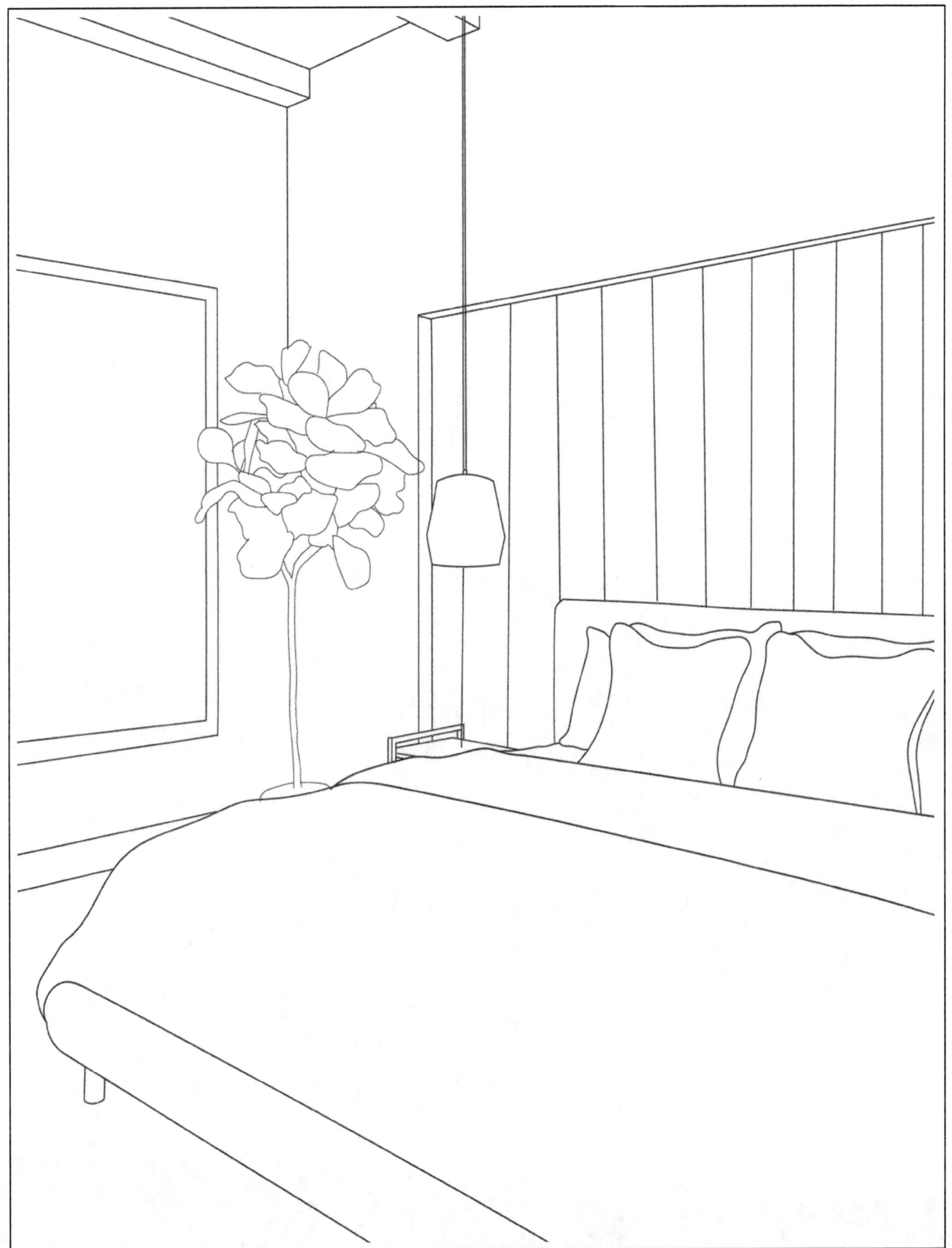

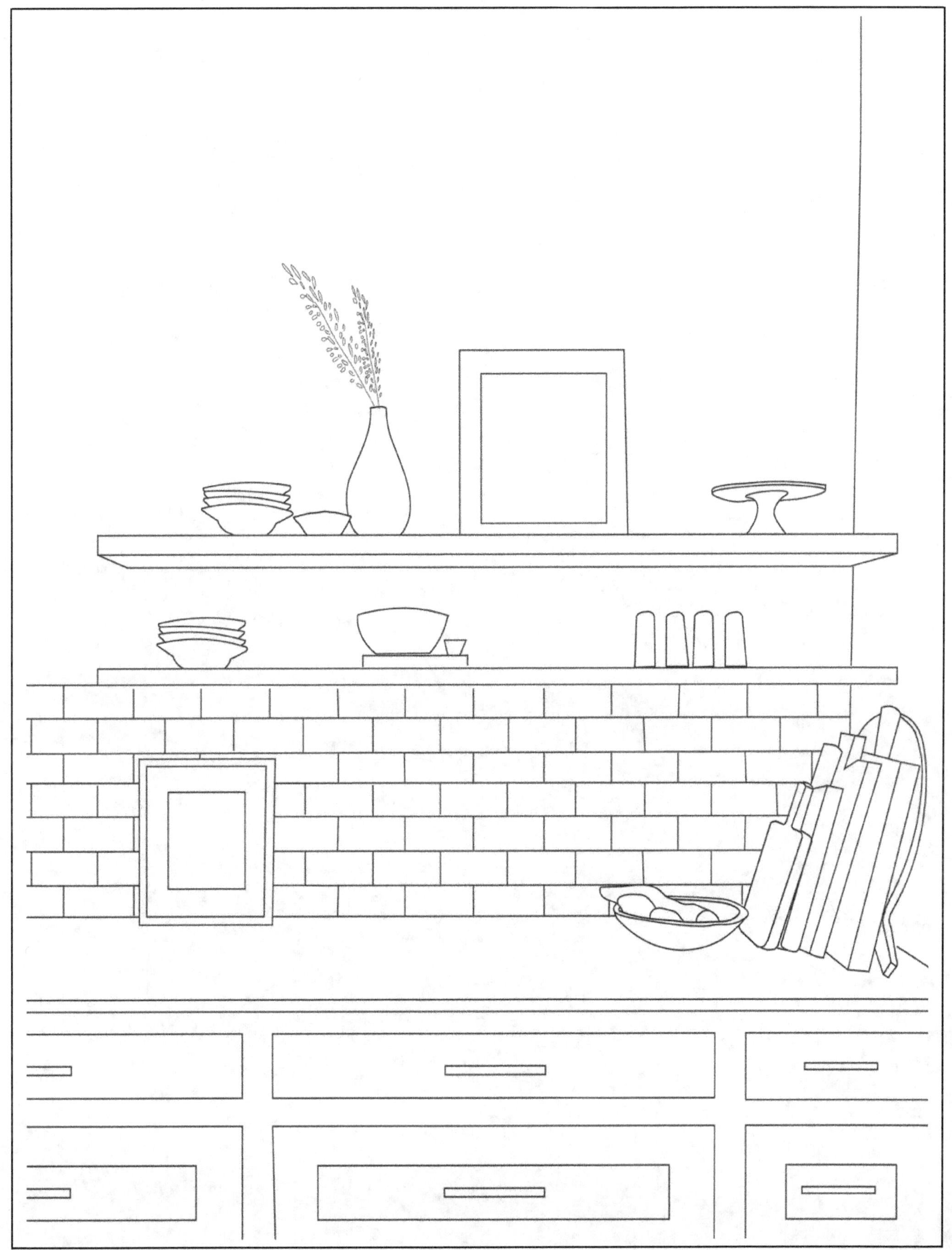

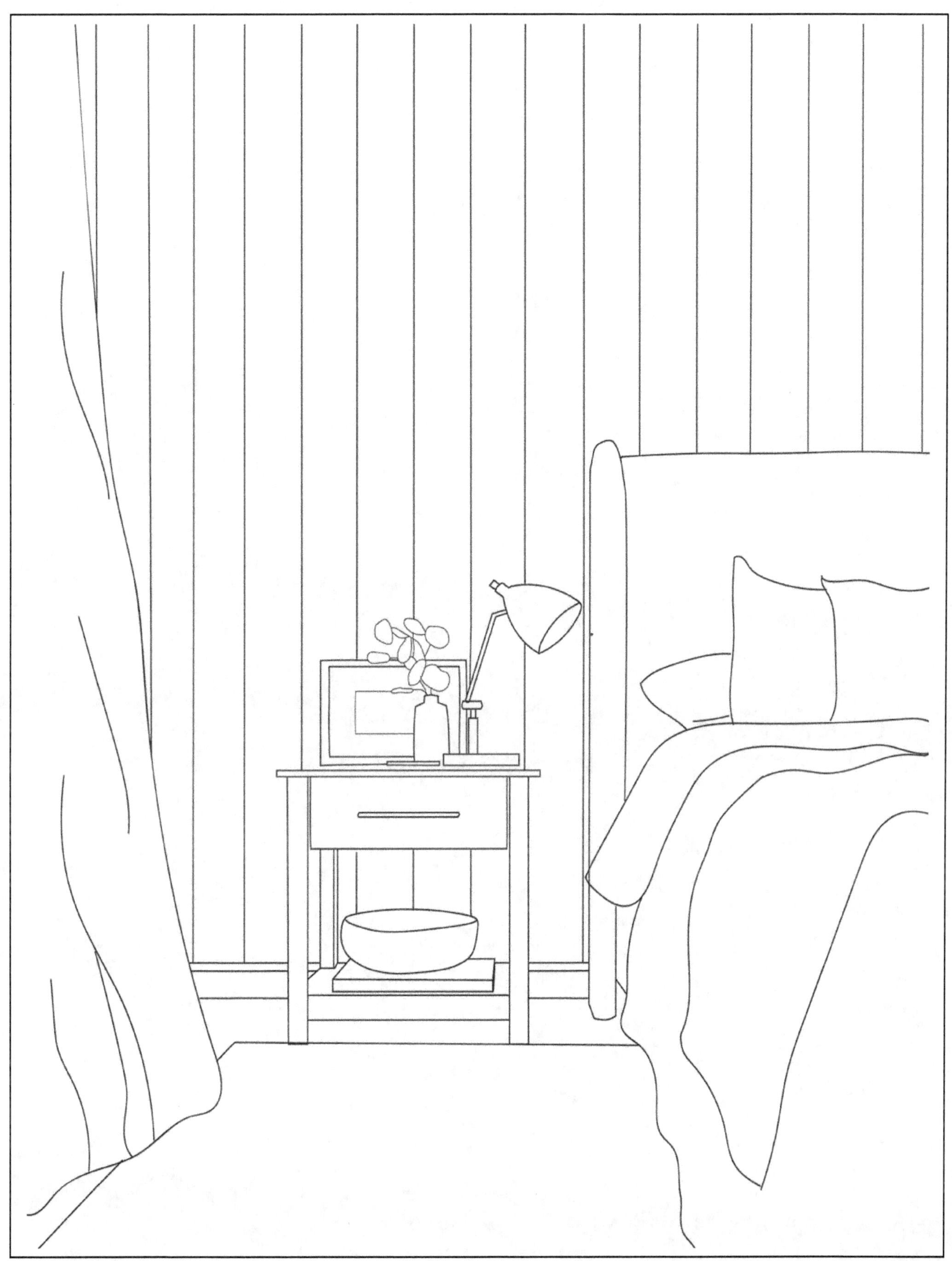

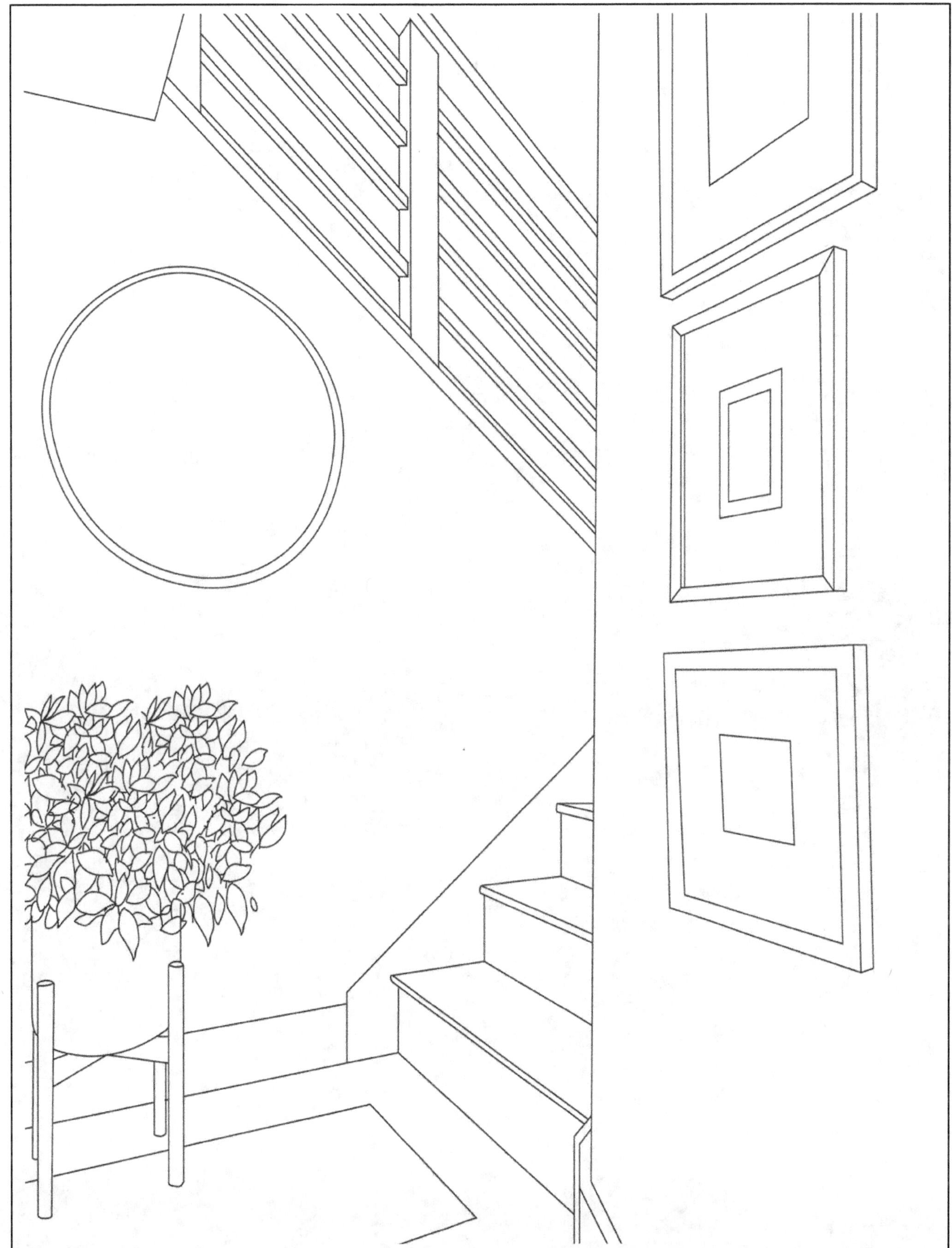

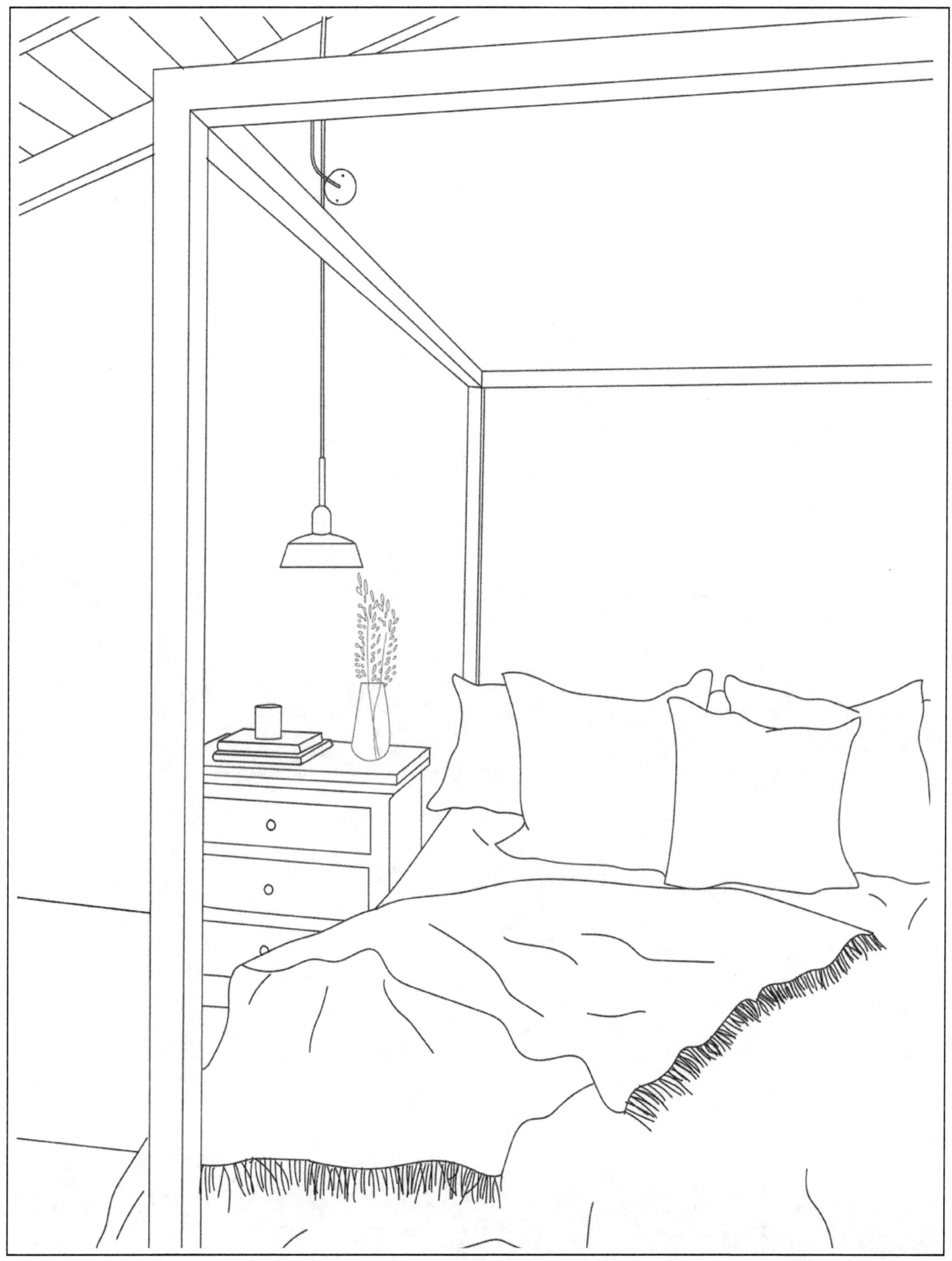

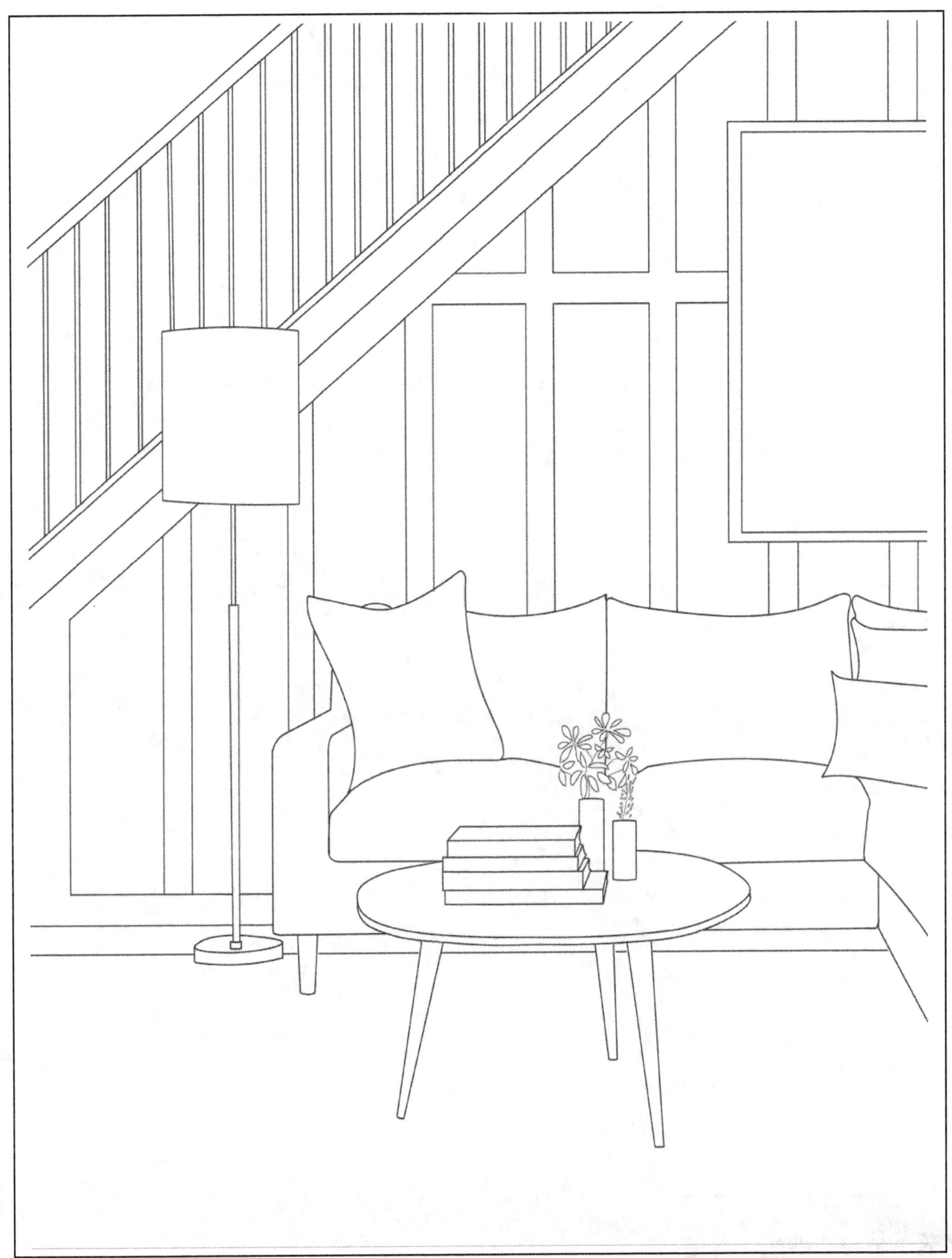